# LOVE AND VARIATIONS

**Carole Satyamurti** is a poet and sociologist who lives and works in London. She teaches at the University of East London, and at the Tavistock Clinic, where her main interest is in relating psycho-analytic ideas to the stories people tell about themselves, whether in formal autobiography or everyday encounters. In 1997 she was writer in residence at the University of Sussex, and she has tutored many times for the Arvon Foundation. She is interested in the links between art and poetry and, with Gregory Warren Wilson, has run workshops at the National Gallery and the Tate Gallery.

She won the National Poetry Competition in 1986, and pub-lished four books of poetry with Oxford University Press: *Broken Moon* (1987), *Changing the Subject* (1990), *Striking Distance* (1994) and *Selected Poems* (1998). The first and third of these books were Poetry Book Society Recommendations. Her latest collection is *Love and Variations* (Bloodaxe Books, 2000).

Copies of Carole Satyamurti's *Selected Poems* are available from Bloodaxe Books.

# CAROLE SATYAMURTI

# *Love*

## *and*

# *Variations*

BLOODAXE BOOKS

Copyright © Carole Satyamurti 2000

ISBN: 1 85224 526 3

First published 2000 by
Bloodaxe Books Ltd,
P.O. Box 1SN,
Newcastle upon Tyne NE99 1SN.


Bloodaxe Books Ltd acknowledges
the financial assistance of Northern Arts.

Cover printing by J. Thomson Colour Printers Ltd, Glasgow.

Printed in Great Britain by
Cromwell Press Ltd, Trowbridge, Wiltshire.

# Acknowledgements

Acknowledgements are due to the editors of the following publications in which some of these poems first appeared: *Ambit, Epoch* (USA), *Frogmore Papers, Hazy Moon, Illuminations, London Magazine, The Observer, Orbis, Oxford Magazine, PEN New Writing* (1996), *Poetry London Newsletter, Poetry Review, PN Review, Psychotherapy Review, The Review* (Vancouver), *The Rialto, Smiths Knoll, Soundings, Stand, Thumbscrew* and *Yale Review.*

# Contents

# 1  *Recorded Delivery*

# Hands
*(for Martin)*


Five hundred miles
have wiped out the patterns
at your finger-ends,
the warm pockets of your palms.
I can't picture your hands

but I know they are
the bass line of a madrigal;
springboard that lets me go;
ample weight-bearing branches;
straight-furrowing plough.

Sometimes they look at each other
– don't they – and see
an insufficient thing.
But they're a Shaker rocking-chair,
beauty and use balancing.

They're a quilt that's right
for every season; deep box
of preserved fruits; my elbow room;
map of the awkward universe;
the sight of home.

## I'll Show You My House

Don't bring politeness, just allowances.
Some of these objects stand outside taste.
They inhabit histories of love

– the pink chair, for instance,
insisting like a boil on being noticed;
though the two-star hotel wallpaper,

the liquorice curtains winking and sneering
'wrong! wrong!' took me many hours
and twice as many dogged miles to find.

Your flawless eye is bound to see
the dross of accumulation like a thickening
around the waist. That's age for you.

Yes, it is always as tidy as this.
I haven't hidden – much. Here,
I'll fling open cupboard doors –

read the contents. Can you tell
how, for years, my affairs have been waiting
to be found in perfect order? I know which

three things I'd snatch if I had to run.
These are the bland and smiling rooms
of someone who's adept at surfaces.

Only – you should see my other rooms,
how cavernous they are, cobwebbed, cluttered;
ah, my invisible rooms are a different storey.

# Like This

If I were in love with you
I'd flit from room to room, like this.

I'd stare into the mirror, baffled,
to search out what you see.

My thoughts would go missing,
like this, would be found drawn

like iron filings to the magnet
that is the fact of you;

and all the weight of old loss
would surface like a wreck

to haunt me, making my skin
crawl with fear, like this.

I'd hallucinate you everywhere
– every letter, phone call, knock,

like this, from you, from you!
If I were in love with you

I'd write a poem, as truthful
as I could; tear it up. Not like this.

# A Dream of Eloquence

Every word-shaped space was spoken for
in that dream emporium of men's wear,
place of artfully arranged mirrors

where you were trying on startled tweeds,
a figured kimono, suit with Grimaldi trousers,
and I was a stone spectator.

Your own clothes were deep blue stripes
of silk velvet, in-sewn with silver thread.
I was consumed by each detail; mute.

Later, at a party – yours, I think –
double glass divided me from all
the shiny conversations, iceberg lives,

until an arm around me brought me
(from dumb despair, not bravery)
to the point when, taking it as yours,

I reached out – fingers docking
between your knuckles – and there
was a place for what I had to say.

# Opal

You've given me all elements but one, in this stone
translated from its origins to hang above my desk
on a gold thread: rhis brilliant angelfish,
drawn from the dark reef of your duffle bag.

Its colours scorch my veins: fuchsia, Antarctic ice.
Staring, I begin to see blood in it as well as beauty,
flame in anguished conversation with itself.
This is yours, and mine; and neither – an oracle.

If we became less vivid to each other, it could
turn filmy like a dying eye. But, then, would we
care; or remember that, once, it swung by a thread
– fire, water, air – into lamplight, into shadow?

# Muse

Don't let's welcome love
in the sweaty horizontals of the bed
– not that again. Enough
of being stapled to the sheets,
disposing surplus limbs.

Listen. Imagine music
– a czardas, say – and we
stand, eyes closed, still.
I can feel the bass
throb in your clavicle.

Look at me. I used to fear
your smile was so charming
that you must lie and lie with it.
You do. And don't.
I find you in the difference.

Give me your hands. With these
few, fine, articulate inches,
couldn't we describe
the otherwise impossible:
love, re-conceived?

It won't come in facile ways,
nor by anxious striving,
but by entering the condition
of a bell, patient for sound,
prepared to fill and fill.

## My Wilderness

Landlocked, imagining licence to discover
the entire reach of you, island by island,
I think of early travellers. It wasn't men

whose medium was ink, paint or stone
who risked life for the literal, but people
who couldn't find a vessel for their dreams.

They would have started with prosaic tasks,
hustling and preparation; slipping out
in fair weather, prudently provisioned;

knowing where they were at first, then sailing
over the world's edge – though sea is sea,
its dangerous temperament at least familiar.

Wouldn't their hearts have thundered in their ribs
at the colossal cragginess of land,
fantasy, massed at the horizon's swell,

now irredeemably external?
What had kept them constant until then
was all they could envision but not yet touch:

all the sharp particulars of awe,
shimmering landscapes, demons and grotesques
that made the formed and formless *Wonderful.*

Hadn't they hoped to be transformed, until
imaginaries of ecstasy and fear
shrank, with the first scrape of keel on sand?

But as they opened up the wilderness
– staked out, mapped, collected, sketched – perhaps,
despite such rich empirical delights,

they paused to think how much more animate
had been their dream-creatures, their Fortunate Isles;
and found they couldn't quite remember them.

# On Not Writing a Letter from Iona

When, after all those jolts and nearly lost connections,
you reach your island – mist, perhaps, swirling milk
along the shore – and you sit at the window, stillness settling
slowly, days stretched out before you like clean canvasses;
when you remember how, a world away, you said
'I'll write', said it deliberately, yet, now, wonder
how you could have been so profligate;
know that I'll receive silence from you
as though it were a letter, and be glad, seeing
there can always be letters, while even small
stacks of days like clean canvasses are precious, few.

## Past Lives

You were a sequinned fish,
and I the glancing light
that could have missed you.

I was a lake you dived into
sending secret shock waves
outwards, without limit.

We were almond trees,
blossoming in sight of one another,
redstarts trafficking between us.

And birds ourselves – thrushes
not too proud for trial runs
at what we'd get so right.

You were a potter
at Jingdezhen, and I
a pear-shaped celadon

wine bottle, forming,
knowing itself inevitable,
under your hands.

## Blue Linen Poem

It buttonholed me in Bond Street,
this poem, the colour of original love.
It seemed meant for you

though, for all I know,
blue linen poems are in mysterious
bad taste – and yours is definitive.

But let it persuade you – turn it
in the light; it is many blues – midnight,
flax, lapis lazuli – each the most beautiful.

When you wear it, feel my arm round you,
my hand skimming your ribs,
delighting in the way you're made.

Wear it – it will sing to you.
In a pocket you may find a chocolate walnut,
or a heart, wrapped, not to stain.

# Bateau-Lit

At five a.m., the room is stretching;
the bed, a creaking boat adrift

on the choppy, grey, Mondrian sea
at the Tate, the one perplexing me

into banal remarks when you,
behind me, in one perfectly surprising

movement, neither insistent nor
tentative, folded me against you

removing us to a different plane,
as if you were that sea, and I, a gull

riding the calm tide of your breath,
not quite in synchrony. We stood

yet were easeful as when we lay
cloud-gazing on a broad green slope

above London, with nowhere to fall,
freed from making grown-up faces,

and just were, not so much talking
as dreaming in the presence of the other

until sky seemed earth, and we hovered
over ice-floes in a sea of inky milk

– and remembering springs me out
onto dry land, to write you this.

## Semi-Precious

You tell me about moonstones,
chosen in India for someone else.
For yourself, a rope of coral.
No jewels for me – but on this page
you are giving me a gift of language,
restringing corals as they might be
the letters of my name; wearing me,
salt to salt, against your skin.

# Water Marks

If I painted you, I'd take brushfuls of sea,
my palette embracing every water colour.
I'd give you million-sequinned skin,
hair, wild and shiny sea-grasses,
flanks, vaulting curves of glass.

But your chest, horizon level, would be
ambiguous as the warm south,
with its own repertoire of distances –
since you are made of sea-stuff, depth
charged with secrets, teeming with gifts.

                    *

Let's play – you be white horses, I'll be
a guillemot riding your dancing shoulders.
You be the spring tide, I'll be limestone
caves you flood with jubilation.

You, the beleaguered Bosphorus,
I, thick fog swathing you in silence;
and a pilot ship who's learned
from experience your intricate shoals.

You be breakers, I'll be sand,
heaping my life up to the water mark,
the dissolving line dividing
dry from drowning.

# Le Mer

'Did you know,' I said, 'Debussy
wrote the last bars of Le Mer
in Eastbourne?' '*La* Mer', you said.

I know very well it's 'la'. La la la!
I've never said 'le mer' before. Ever.
I'm aware of those critical

moments when the scales shift,
lustre tarnishes a little: those
small desponding irreversibles.

So what blind urge to test
your love's capaciousness, what fit
prompted me to offer you 'Le Mer'?

## On Not Being Impulsive

Posting my letter through your door
I caught, through red stained glass, a sight
of you, back from your travels, reading
at the kitchen table; and it seemed right

that you should be roseate like that,
and I, seeing you – one glance all
I needed to preserve you: a glowing
lozenge in my nocturnal hall.

Ah, but I was tempted to knock,
being mad to hold you for a minute,
just that; to know your bone-and-muscle
realness, after so long; and hated it,

hated that this most natural thing
(just then, more longed for than any
words) would have been – wouldn't it? –
one knock, one hug, one minute too many.

# Heartmarks

This frail-looking balustrade,
all that stood between us and certain
death on the paving-stones below,
is where we first touched without
a spun glass reticence between us.

That Soho market...this revolving door...
the layout of the city is peppered
with such places. To fix them
with precise coordinates of words
would arrest their gauzy meanings,

but on the map described by memory
you'll find me whirling nightly
from Bertaux to Pimlico, haunting
Long Acre, Kenwood, Gabriel's Wharf:
all the stations of love.

## All This, You Give Me

You've drawn me into your medium
of light and lightness. Resisting closure,
all the bulky furniture of love,
you bring me, heart pounding every time,

into huge rooms, stripped of fixtures,
where you let me find you, lose you,
invent you from scraps of light;
our ways intersect in great ellipses.

This is new ground, but we move easily
from earth to air, earth to imagination.
Oh, I'll never fly like that, but I swing with you,
catch your trapeze of glistening filaments.

Knowing you makes me weep sometimes,
as strong sunlight does; the taste of lemons.
I'm learning to ride your necessary silences.
I breathe you in, airborne grains of gold.

You have en-lightened me, taught me that love
is unhoardable as air; the moment, all there is.
You show me what eyes are for. Loving you,
I gaze, weightless, at the spinning world.

# Forgiveness

Waiting at regret's causeway to nowhere,
I was cast out from my natural harbour,
a ghost boat, pain-restless under the plausible veneer.

There was a scrounging robin, and daffodils,
bobbing inanely, flaunted their excess of yellow
indifferent to how I'd angered you, appalled myself.

Then you, walking across the hill to meet me halfway
and suddenly I was berthed in your arms
where past and future flowed into a now

suspended perfectly, words surrendered
and we, resolved – I streaming water, you
breath, fire, earth welcoming me home.

Yet how could I, apprentice in the cross-grained
discipline of love, receive absolution from you simply,
how be completely comforted, knowing I must fail, and fail?

# Rewind

Today, you would have got my letter
saying, 'In the garden, a blackbird
is singing, *je veux dire, je veux dire.*
I want to say – I mean – can you come?'

Thousands of streets away, you see my writing
reach out – then fall back, as the envelope
levitates, is sucked back through the letterbox
into pouch, van, sorting frame,

is re-bagged at Mount Pleasant, hurtles
through Kentish fields, skips the Channel,
drops like quicksilver down the map of France
– Le Mans, Tours, Poitiers, Angoulême –

to where I know the impatient timbre
of the postman's engine, how long he takes
to place a letter in the small metal box,
from which I tweak it; and begin again.

# For Want of a Better Thing

Instead of speech, here is a letter.
No, instead of a letter, here is a poem,
and if the poem were you it would be
wrapped in a silver coat, washed
in Himalayan meltwater. This poem
would return you to yourself, annealed.

You're not here for me to feed you,
my fierce and gentle swan. I can't
offer you the bowl of my lap,
nor be a fulcrum for you. This
is my possible speech, letter, poem.
What do I have but words to love you in?

## 'Are There Birds?'

The birds here are invisible to me,
flying on the safe side, in this country
where men shoot small birds for sport.

I hear them – cuckoo, finches' sweet
needle-point of sound, the sharp derision
of a woodpecker; and the nightingale's

nightly soliloquy in the sinister red prunus
whose leaves are being cast off – in May.
Superstitious, I want it to behave seasonably

but, much more, I want there to be
birds visible, to describe them to you;
vivid, remarkable ones, so you will come.

Since they're your natural kin – quick,
felicitous, conditioned not to trust – perhaps
they'll appear for you, settle near:

a palette of birds, an enchantment of acrobats,
an illuminated library of feathered volumes
speaking for me. So you will stay.

**II** *Boy with a Fish*

# Boy with a Fish

*(in memoriam SCM: 1944-1995)*

## 1

For your funeral, we pin pictures of you
on a board. To revive you,

to assure ourselves light fell on you once,
smiler, joker. Blown egg.

Larking on a beach: cardboard playboy
in tilted Bogart panama, white twill;

the wedding (we're unsure, but choose it
for that frail joy, part of the story).

No recent ones. Everyone stares hardest
at this one: aged fourteen, perhaps,

hefting an enormous bream you'd caught.
You look at us, hold out the fish,

shoulders hunched, offering.

**2**

*Is that all – why aren't you top?*
Father's bloodstock, his future winner.
He named his cabin-cruiser after you.

He shinned down the cliff of figures
like an alpinist. *See, it's easy!*
You, mute, swallowing his pride.

What did you take from your expensive schooling
but appearances? You couldn't allow
anyone to teach you anything. Never would.

Now, thinking of my rare, dutiful
enquiries from my side of the city,
I hear your cadence: *Nothing. Nobody.*

**3**

Come to clear the flat, we're clinging
to each other's common sense, to words
positioned carefully, like hand-holds.

The smell, a substance
invading even thought:
rotten food, unwashed skin.

Overwhelming waste. All furniture
engulfed by takeaways,
thousands of crushed tissues,

ruined clothes, three years'
newspapers, Marlboro packets, butts,
ash on ash on ash.

Only the telephone stands clear,
and beside it, placed, poems of mine
I don't know if you read.

This black bed, where they found you
comatose, blankets ravaged by mice
whose nests we startle: small, energetic lives.

Held in the light, even our most extreme
nightmares can become mere narratives.
There ought to have been words instead of this.

**4**

What draws tears isn't chaos,
but this mirror by the door
where you must have checked,
tidied your hair with this brush,
squared your shoulders, practised
that cellophane expression.
Then walked out to the street
and become invisible.

## 5

In masks and gloves,
like asbestos workers,
we bag up, bundle, scrub,
disinfect, retreating only
when dust grabs us by the throat.

Brutal, we pile stuff high in the yard,
call in the Council.
The house clearance man
offers twenty quid for everything.

Out go the ebony elephants,
a hundred unused guitar strings,
a lifetime's easy listening.

After three days, we have clean surfaces,
four stripped rooms, stinging with Dettol.

The estate agent talks prices. Talks *desirable*.

**6**

Your names were a three-piece suit.
The first, formal;
the second, father's heavy hand-me-down;

the surname, unusual, allowing
entry to the family romance:
the castle on the Borders.

You could have grown into it.
Father couldn't wait for that,
scornful when you tripped.

You learned a way of seeming,
tricked yourself out – elegance,
reckless generosity.

Time stained it. But it was
your last proud possession,
final covering.

## 7

How does a man get by with a skin too few?
He keeps very still,
so still, he can hear the surge of his blood as it travels;
so still, he discovers himself saying *no* in his sleep.

No attachment, no lurch of hope or ambition
leads him to reach out,
fearful of splits and cracks. Sensation is bandaged.
He treads with the delicacy of a tight-rope walker

but attracts no admiring audience. He gathers himself
in a tatterdemalion rig-out
– habit, bravado, blind-alley facts – too ill-fitting
to keep out the cold. A garment that passes for skin.

8

Where did you put your self?

Not, lately, into work, though you had thrived
on office life, settled for peanut wages:
a tacit trade-off for the times you'd ring in
sick, or not turn up, after your benders.

Not into love. Was it belief in magic
(*gullible*, we reckoned, even then)
sent you spinning into marriage with
a girl you met in Tenerife? How soon

the disappointments mounted. Then she left,
taking the sapphire ring, the better linen,
draining your non-renewable resource
of confidence: *you're not a proper man.*

And not into these diaries: twenty years
of 'Mum rang', 'dentist', 'signed on', 'paid the gas',
what you ate, the occasional 'dirty evening'.
Where are you? In the silences.

**9**

I remember you new born,
a squashy thing between your legs
– something wrong!

Mother didn't put me right.
You were the son father longed for.
Later on, she'd say

you were too much like her,
as though some softness,
lack of drive, had been

passed down; no amount
of love enough to cancel out
her early luke-warm welcome.

Sitting with you those days of coma,
marking your laboured breath,
I see a wrong key in the lock.

**10**

Scorpio. In mid-October,
you joked about the big Five-O –
*bring on the zimmer frame* – and talked
of *one or two odd jobs* around the flat
you never let us into. Sometimes,
I knew you were there, not answering.

That week at mother's, wanting the day
witnessed, you sounded bright, excited,
as though, at fifty, you'd be a man
of substance, with meaning in your wallet.

I don't know how it went. Soon, that place
received you back. So far beyond odd jobs.
Only five months for you to follow
your defeated fern, uncomplaining,
into the dark.

## 11

Love has struck me as a painful fact
I didn't know I knew. We couldn't cope
with saying it, but wrote, phrase-book fashion,
'Dearest S', 'Lots of…', 'XXX';
word packages we took care not to open.

What shocks me now is love's tenacity.
I think of the Rose of Jericho, its dour
tangle blossoming in rain. As strange,
after such stubborn drought, for the heart
to yield this piercing, anachronistic flower.

## 12

When she said, *It's all right, darling,*
*everything's going to be all right now,*
stroking your head, I'm certain
you heard her – the bone-familiar
voice that gave you birth, releasing you.

Poses, lies, bigotry, every awkward edge
– all your life's pitiful distractions –
slid from you then. In death, you became
more than material – pharoah, famine victim,
soldier, the dead, grey Christ. Every human.

# III  *Surface Tension*

# Leasehold

Does everyone think this – one day I'll knock
at that childhood house, where trespassers now live,
and ask to see? But never do, shrinking
from too little, or too much, recall,
anxious to protect our box of shadows.

One winter evening, dressed in black,
I hitched open that same sticking gate
into the garden I'd not seen for decades.
Skirting the garage (no queasy Humber)
I came on the house, off guard and somnolent.

These were the dusk-colours of a photograph:
here I'd perfected the flip of stolen currants
from palm to mouth; and on that window-sill
risked a glassy death to read the night sky
for God's expression, his take on my fractured world.

Drawn to the one lighted window, I felt
– not nostalgia, it wasn't home I longed for
but for a second, reparative, twist
at turning points, the chance to etch a different
mark in that gas-fumed hallway, on those stairs.

                              *


Now, about to leave another house
on an open-ended journey, the idea ,
*departure,* awes me – its solemnity,
and time leaching, making my skin prickle.
I try to hold it in a net of tasks.

*Après moi…* Lately, I dream I've come
back here to find doors hung on empty air,
rooms crumpled in on themselves
like toothless mouths. Stout walls pulverise
without my living life to nourish them.

I've occupied this chain of rooms as if
creating something permanent, the colours,
temperatures and light to love in, work in.
To be alone in – coming back at night
from the clamorous proximities of the city

to hear the door's sweet, self-sufficient click,
the healing silence. This is happiness:
a crowded tableful of friends I've brought
together, like the best ingredients, scatter,
talking still, into the street, and I

apply myself to the companionable
clutter – my order, my domain again.
And yet, the plumbing's gurgling irony
reminds me: the house is self-possessed.
Irrelevant, fastidious whites and ochres,

my gracefully shaped arch. Reversible.
The house, indifferent to taste, retains
its skeleton; and I, vain freeholder,
am little else but frivolous breath on glass,
the transient impress of foot and hand.

We're interchangable, we occupants.
In the small hours, sometimes boundaries slip.
A noise wakes you – a creaking joist, is it?
The springing of a catch? Silence. Then
someone's breathing somewhere in the room;

the walls are throbbing. Harsh, tense breaths
approaching very near. Dark is felt-thick;
You will yourself blockish as timber.
In those seconds, you travel a whole life-time
before you know the breathing as your own.

*

Lists, algorithms, long-term instructions,
all the will's scaffolding – as if sheer diligence
could painlessly tie up all ends and leave
no life-long conversations gaping
with all that's still to say, and won't be now.

Real time's run out; even a meta-list
won't hold me up. If I don't come back
they'll peel every room, skin by skin,
tissues of meaning loosened from their backing
to re-form, wander, settle where they can.

Will someone glance inside my notebooks?
All the lines and fragments – will they leap out
like clowns, assassins, suitors, militants?
Or, malnourished orphans, slip the page?
Words, the last skin; beyond them, nothing.

# Les Autres *or* Mr Bleaney's Other Room

Hell is a hotel bedroom. Other people,
implicit in the trapped, pine-freshened air,
fill you with their discomforts – room not quite
warm enough, bed intolerant. It's clear

you're one of a sad company who've seen
themselves summed up by chintz and candlewick,
who've spat in this basin, interrogated this
same toilet bowl for signs; or, maybe, sick

of their own company, turned on TV
and tried to feel drama or panel game
might give a purchase on some richer life,
but found the room immured them just the same.

You, like them, lie squeamish on the sheet
that veils the map of other people's lust,
fever, clumsiness, incontinence;
toss, sleepless and resentful, under musty

blankets' meagre weight, and realise
how you have buttressed your identity
with fragile props, convinced yourself of your
uniqueness. Foolish. You'll see – when you die

you'll land up in the final hotel bedroom,
where your mucus, dandruff, pubic hairs and sweat
will (but for the finer print of DNA)
turn out to be like anyone's you've met;

and though to swallow your disgust and breathe
deeply the air you share with everyone,
as if you loved them, might transform a hell
into a kind of heaven – can it be done?

## Leaving Present

The ritual clock: you've done your time,
now's the time for the time of your life,
for all the time in the world. You place
the clock where it can see you.

Time's always come in blocks. Now
it floods the landscape of your days,
effacing the old boundaries.
Your purposes dissolve in it.

Time keeping's as unnecessary
as you are, but you're shackled to
this bland-faced border-guard,
its smug and vacuous syllabics

prophesying mean time,
injury time, time out of mind,
the moment when your time
is up, is up, is up.

# The Woman Nextdoor

*(for Susan Wicks)*

At 3 a.m., the sky rips open; fury
beats on the slates, hammers the windows.
The drains gag on excess.

Wind, shrieking in a foreign language,
jackboots the door, beside itself;
lightning searches every corner.

I know my neighbour's roof leaks,
that she must be madly juggling
with bowls; deprived of sleep.

I tuck the duvet round me.
The rain is being hurled
by some unreasoning power.

She should have had it fixed.
She's like that. We each have phones.
I have a spare bed. She's probably

shifting to the dry side of hers,
clinging to the edge...
Broom, yellow plastic dustpan,

float, clatter against furniture.
The water rises, lifts her, hurtles her
out, over the drowned garden,

down to the valley bottom,
where the road's a river;
and I spot her, in the sensible

pyjamas I've seen on the line,
rotating, tossing like a log, until
she's swept into the woods,

and I lose her...At 10 a.m.,
her curtains are still closed.
I sit on the terrace

in rinsed pearl light,
eating fresh bread, reading
that book by Eva Fogelman.

# The Jew of Chantérac

Back then, no one would have called him that. No feature, no practice,
no seven-branched candlestick, no distinctiveness marked him,
not even his name – not Lévi but Demartin, not Mordecai but Jacques.

Did someone with a gun at their throat, and a son in the Maquis, seize
a wisp of hope – as one might try to soft-soap an ordinary bully,
as *I'll take you to where there are otters,* or something else rare and
        harmless?

Or, out of no special grievance, no previous sense of difference,
into the mouth of some citizen who'd always been anxious to please
and couldn't stop now; or into a mind sharp for self-advancement

sprang Jacques, his name already a tempting sop to throw
the Gauleiter, who snapped him up, although demanding
tribute more abundant than a single, peaceable Jew.

But later, no one wanted to rake over who'd said what;
and because the white-veiled girls were shut up in the church and burned;
and the boys in their Sunday clothes were rounded up and shot

he hardly counts. So although each year, even now, people
cram into the church to honour the names of those who could have been
more to them, teenage great-uncles and aunts, there's no memorial

to the man in the cobbler's shop who turned out to be a Jew,
to the way they shouted and spat; to the ancient sway of his back
as he stuffed things into a case, enough for a week or two.

What remained of him after he'd gone north-east up the narrow-gauge
        track?
An increasingly abstract guilt in some elderly breast? Vague stories.
A small gap: there's never since been a Jew in Chantérac.

# Sunset Over Tottenham Hale

Gospel Oak to Barking, Barking to Gospel Oak:
the usual pleasures of the grubby train that shuffles
me to work and back include sinful snacks

novels in day-time. But not the raw
heaps of graveyard steel, urban farm
where everything moults in despair.

Nor terrace fronts whose every brick
is picked out in shaky black, or encrusted
from ground to eaves in multi-coloured mosaic.

My throat aches at the patience of it;
I think of my own, equally convinced, aesthetic.
Then, today, nature took sides and elected kitsch

throwing a vast canopy of flamy tatters
over the flatlands of east London. Brick,
glass, concrete reflected glory; altostratus

streaming in Strictly Ballroom rose,
Cartland mauve, Metro Goldwyn carmine
and russet – a brash brass band of a blaze.

At first, no one looked, but stared stiffly
at newspapers, slumped as if too full
of trouble to be touched; or as if

every day, Canary Wharf stood like a survivor
of *blitzkrieg*, and the sky spread out such gifts.
But then first one face then others came alive,

smiles passed between us as a flood
of copper, spilling across the reservoirs,
transformed greasy grey to dragon's blood.

# The Life and Life of Henrietta Lacks

That was me in the New Look
sassy as hell, in the days
when wicked was wicked;
not the fist on hip of a woman
who knows she's cooking
a time bomb tumour;

not a number's up smile
like a dame who figures
she'll not be getting the wear
from all those yards
of cloth she scrimped for,
who'll be dead at thirty.

Dead? For forty years
my cloned cervical cells
have had a ball in Petri dishes
gorging placenta soup,
multiplying like their crazy mother
– the first ever cell line,

flung like spider's thread
across continents I never got to visit,
the stuff of profits, reputations
from Melbourne to Baltimore;
hot property, burning mindless
energy I'd have known how to use.

They never asked. Never said
*How's about you live for ever,*
*like immortal yogurt?* I'm bought,
sold like cooking fat. But I get even,
grow where I'm not supposed,
screw up experiments.

Soon, they'll have the know-how
to rebuild me from a single cell.
A rope of doubles could jitterbug
from here to Jupiter. Meantime,
I'm grabbing my piece of the action,
hungry to cry my first cry again.

# The Front

In old age, when the land begins to tilt, they roll
like marbles, gently, towards the coast, coming to rest
in condominiums with impatient gardens, and rules.

Here, washing lines, ragged cries of pain
are unacceptable. Here are brave faces, a glaze
of gentle manners. The past curls up behind them.

Promenade punctuates their mornings, those aches
affirming one's still there. They step out,
troupers, earning the comfort of hot chocolate,

fighting to hold the line against decay with camouflage,
cunning, with not naming parts that can't be helped.
They can dance, can swing an iron, and are doing it

for all of us – up ahead, acting impervious
to tides and weather, to show how one can smile
beside that slippery remembrancer, the sea.

# Freedom of the City

Office blocks like silver-suited posers
are mirrors for each other. All day, weather
glides across their beautiful, blank faces.

Below, you scurry in pursuit of choices –
this film or that, what kind of food, which jacket
will suit you best, and is it still in fashion?

And underlying those, the other questions –
how are you doing, where is it you're heading,
who will you be today? For you are never

your own whole story. It doesn't take some clever
dick in the Sorbonne to show you what
a circus of selves you are. It's a pleasure

to give them an airing, since you have the leisure
to be *flâneuse*, mark, rent-a-crowd...though thinking,
as you drop a coin in some young man's guitar case –

is his face, turned blankly to yours, is your face
so different, after all, from what's above:
the play of surface on another surface?

# Birthmark

Sun throws my shadow onto the stone bench
and within it are lichens: ashy green, ochre,
scabby home to blood red micro-beetles.

Insistence, grip, their greed for *lebensraum*
have mapped this sandstone with a pointillist
scatter of colonies, macular settlements

draining colour from their hinterland:
these, the townships of Natal, and these
the farms and homesteads of my ex-pat uncles.

My silhouette incorporates them.
They make me sin ugly, give me features
I shall own, until cloud erases me.

# The Blessing
*(for Sidney Buckland)*


Suddenly
a flying pair of compasses
described desperate parabolas
through the room,
buffeting bookcases,
scrabbling for purchase,
terror terrified.

A rush of purpose, then,
arrowed it for sunlight,
dashed it against
the puzzle of unyielding air
to a stunned thump on the floor.

I took it outside,
folded its rumpled wings.
It was still. But blinked, blinked,
as if to reassess a world
where matter could be this deceitful.

Such nearness was peculiar.
I stroked its back
with a slow, humming finger.
It cocked its head,
looked left, right, then
launched off;
instantly, just one more sky diver.

Might it not carry, though,
some organic trace
of being comforted
– as I will, of being
shaken by frantic flight;
palpitating blue?

## Spring Offensive

May's the month for optimistic acts:
seedlings – pansies, stocks, geraniums –
bedded in, gauche first-day-at-schoolers.
Your thumbs have blessed them, inner eye furnishing
dowdy beds with dazzling coverlets.

Through the lengthening dusk, snail battalions
creep on prehensile bellies from their dugouts.
They bivouac around your bright hopes,
slurp rich juices; vandal lace-makers
growing fat on your would-be colours.

You stumble out at dawn and catch them at it,
scrawling silver sneers on wall and path,
and snatch them from their twigs, impervious to
their endearing horns, their picture-bookness.
You crush them, or worse, lay down poisonous snacks.

Yet aren't their shells as lovely as petunias,
patterned like ceramic works of art
from a more coherent age? And might they not
defend with slow, tenacious argument
their offspring, soon to fizz and drown in salt?

Summer's on their side. Each night, new recruits
will graduate from dark academies.
You lie plotting extravagant revenges.
Asleep, you're in a world where, very slowly,
children, friends, are running out of air.

# Pentecost

A constant tumble downstream
presses through a slight narrowing
and produces not steady sound
but an altercation between water
and water, water and stone.
Gulping laughter as the river
clears its throat and passes on,
slipping through watercresses
that resist what must be,
this perpetual escape,
as if drenched in such fixed nostalgia
they can't welcome the continual new.

A storm rising, and the field of rye,
knowing and not knowing,
stands en bloc, until the wind
gathers itself into a passion,
sweeps among the standing stalks
stirring, harrassing them all ways
until the whole charged field
is a pan of roiling green;
or a palimpsest, bearing
every version of the wind's
rage for expression;
while each plant flexes, weathering.

But it ends like this:
after a day of busyness,
when it has rained, but stopped at last,
and the earth exhales pleasurable breath
at the sun's late reappearance,
two blackbirds release joyful voices
in endlessly inventive antiphons;
praise singers, offering up a line,
catching, re-forming it. And this is
what should be – unconfined ambition,
raising above the stream
a shining ziggurat of sound.

# By the Time You Read This

She's lost her touch with doors
– push or pull almost always wrong.
By such improbabilities, a person
comes to feel chosen for punishment.

Old age must be like this – no point,
walking on stranger's feet,
drawn to the centre of the earth.
Her cheek thumps the pavement.

This is an old sin with a neutral name.
Objects treat her as the enemy she is;
cartons impregnable, taps unyielding,
needle's eye closed against her thread.

*

The scales are constant
but she's become micro-thin,

contained between
two faces of the page.

People write on both sides of her,
the smooth and the smooth;

they think they're
making an impression.

In another room,
a woman is screaming.

Uselessly carrying on.

*

*Remember me.*

*I am marcasite for mother's finger,*
*father's enamelled trophy.*

*I am a gleaner of abandoned shells*
*wasting for the rinse of sea.*

*I am a picture in an exhibition*
*by blind photographers.*

*I am a deaf-mute harnessing vibrations*
*in a pail of pitch.*

*I am a masked crab. Dismember me*
*— discover a cache of shreds.*

# The Perversity of Mirrors

You could spend years of waking hours in front of them
and not catch how, nor exactly when
three-dimensional geometry goes soft on you:
features drawn on a slow-punctured balloon.

Since flesh will never re-compose itself
you want to splash your eyes with indigo,
gloss your teeth fluorescent, your life
made over in epileptic stripes.

Once, I told a man whom I respected
I'd refurbished my house all pink and green
with mirrors everywhere, while I
kept to myself washed terra cotta,

aquamarine, uncluttered walls
in the house he'd never visit – hoping
he'd see through me, such a talent
being part of what I loved in him.

I still regret the throw-away vulgarity
that lodged ugly rooms in his mind's cellar
where I'm mirrored, fairground foolish,
having no hold on what is beautiful.

## Missing You

That you had that smile we'll all remember,
that you had the perfect voice for Gershwin,
that your children are, of course, a credit,
that your wife stands here taut-lipped and tearful

makes the vicar's work easy as he re-frames you
as a deft montage, our take-home present.
Your coffin stands trestled at the altar – and you,
already you're mist, missing in translation.

Yes, you were strong in the defence of dolphins,
but are you content in your padded coat of epithets?
Or will you come to me wearing that other smile
with the thirty-two-in-one wicked meanings?

# Sitting for Manou

Manou is doing my portrait in gouache.
We're in her high studio with the unkind glare,
massed with the prints she sells; her paintings
like jewels, like electricity. As she positions me,

I wonder – how can I, neat and beige
and common as a glove, be transposed
into that intensity. But she is responsible.
She narrows her eyes to shut me in.

Her ritual passes at the canvas,
fencing footwork, her urgent muttering,
are crystallised desire. She makes herself
the channel for what I am, what I am not.

The space between us shimmers like hot tar;
seeing, being seen, a circuit I long to escape
to somewhere safer. But I've signed up
for malaise, this active stillness.

Am I these colours, planes, surfaces?
She labours to bring me to light.
I submit to the uncomfortable squeeze
of being remoulded; and attend the birth.

# Two Quiet Women

Kate P gets into Balliol.
Her friend, Nicole,
who's always been considered dim,
gets in nowhere. Aimless, glum,
she moves to Headington.

Kate's crushed by ex-Etonians,
the way they walk,
the grown-up-baby way they talk.
She dreads tutorials, is getting
phobic about writing,

thinks of suicide. But wait,
it's not too late.
Each week, she and Nicole read,
discuss, then, when they're agreed,
Nicole writes the essay.

Kate's tutor says he is impressed,
although he finds
in between, he can't call her to mind.
Nicole dons subfusc, goes to Schools,
sits Kate's Finals.

Kate gets a starred First. Nicole,
by deed poll,
changes her name to Katherine P.
Kate and Kate, with their degree,
are hot property.

One quiet woman is much like another.
Two quiet women can take on the world and his brother.

# Undine

Come to me, husband, beautiful stupid one, satin-skinned handful;
goat-leap the coast path as though you were running to meet the applause
of ten thousand admirers. I've watched you until it's no longer a pleasure.

Come to my cave. The eddies are sucking on nothing but foretaste
of you, sweet frigate. Now you, too, are wet as the sea, and as eloquent;
cries flood your throat like the rasp and thrash of incoming rollers.

*

I've swallowed you into my future through all my insatiable mouths
– unbearable if you had left as though this were some everyday dalliance,
carelessly vaulting the breakwaters, whistling, smelling of salt.

*

The tide has retreated; the sand is a frowning expanse in the semi-light.
Gulls wheel and seek; their mewling a restless complaint, out of tune
with the listless slap, the sullen, reproachful sigh of the sea.

My love, my bridge to the world of steel cities, of dancing and flight
– why is there pain when I think what I did to you? Why do my eyes
            stream
feeling your monstrous child swim in me, vigorous, mortal as fish?

# Constanze's Wedding

*(for Gregory Warren Wilson)*

### 1

He insisted, not wanting me to take it from politeness:
if I didn't like it – meaning more than like – I should be honest.
I would have been (we have that much easiness between us)
but how would I not love such mouth-watering blue, the mystery
of how the flowers are made, felicities of glass, chased silver?

Later, he told me how, in his Venice room, he'd tried it on,
stared in the mirror to judge if I'd like it, see as he did.
I understood. Every morning I try on my whole body,
dress myself in desire; and he's the mirror, the appraising
eye that sees me, deficient past disguising. Today

when my longing, finally unchecked, will take me to the door
where this beginning ends, what will he make of me? Will he see
what it takes to bring him a gift pierced through with such misgiving?
I'll wear his necklace. They say Venetian glass splits, shivers
when danger touches it. If he doesn't like me, will it know?

### 2

Afterwards, it was as if a carp, too big
for its bowl, threshed this way and that
inside my head. The night turned to marble,
moonlight drained colour from the counterpane.

Had he called me beautiful, I'd have shrunk away
(the ugly sister has the thinnest skin) but once
I'd seen him take up a neglected viola
and felt I understood its joy in realising

its full register, the voice he knew was there.
Now I know I had hoped too specifically.
There was so much I didn't understand
and he said nothing to tell me if I pleased him

so that, after he slept, my body was the hollow
of the bell clanging each quarter; the rumpled linen,
dry cliffs ranged between us, until I heard him
sing in his sleep: *Ach ich liebte, war so glücklich!*

# It's Not the Same

If I say *I love you*, it is not the same
as if you say it.

A pair of Tories cast non-identical votes.
Two ten-year-olds don't murder the same toddler.

Two athletes do not fail the same drugs test.
We each die of a unique disease.

My parents did not live in the same marriage,
swallowed different silent Sunday roasts.

When we share a Granny Smith, you see red,
though we may never know this.

Since last week's cool is this week's boring;
because words are mercury, not bricks;

because a flip remark can change the world;
and the mind is always fidgeting with its own furniture,

you never step into the same jeans twice,
nor out of the same bed, nor into the same poem;

you never play the same favourite track twice,
nor speak the same platitude.

And when I said *I love you*, yesterday,
I meant 'I can feel your attention wandering';

when I say it tomorrow, I may mean,
'I want to see if I believe it when I hear it.'

But today, *I love you* is as almost simple,
is as nearly literal as you'll ever get.

# Jacques Lacan's Table

My table pretends it's solid,
that it's the same table now as yesterday,
that it exists, when I'm not sitting at it.

Once, it shuffled over to the glass
and saw such robust lines and angles,
such harmonies, coherence of design

that it's not been happy since, yearns
for that immaculate, whole tablehood,
transcendence of the quaking flux

of molecules, kaleidoscopic selves,
surface barely able to contain
dizzy plurality.

It seeks comfort from accomplices,
is grateful for a touch of beeswax,
gives me back the image of my hand.

It suits me to collude,
so I load it with books, a pot of coffee,
lean my elbow on it, doing this.

# Love and Variations

Love. No one asked me for it.
No one's fault if hearing
that way of saying 'know',
black ink on thick cream paper,
the scent of crushed gum leaves,
bring this vertigo.

\*

It's like childbirth,
self-inflicted; the way
you let yourself fall;
new life stirring you
to one-track smiles;
the resolve, this time,
to do it differently;
the way, every time,
you forget how it hurts.

\*

I have neuralgia. Or is it?
Restless legs, blurred vision.
At the sound of the telephone
I sweat sheets of ice.
My doctor, sceptical, makes
an ayurvedic pulse diagnosis.
Love, she says. In the circumstances,
an absurd complaint. Not contagious.

\*

This is the fictional house
I've chosen: locked closets,
lovely rooms pleasuring themselves.
Narrow ledges where I try to settle.
I wander among shifting screens
I'd thought were walls, and am lost.

*

Love is *scordatura*;
a cello forgetting itself,
entranced by wilder possibilities;
a C string, insanely

relinquishing its proper pitch.
It is joy breaking into a run
despite the habit of caution,
despite the fault line in the bone.

*

If love's the theme, in the first variation
I'm tuned at awkward intervals;

in the second, I'm playing the wrong part;
we've forgotten all the notes in the third;

but in the fourth we remember, and then
our skins sing like a choir of wine glasses.

*

Sometimes, thinking of him,
I see a hare – not one puppeted
by the somersaults of Spring,
but a hare in Summer, power embodied,

made for *grands jetés*, delighting;
now tensed against incursion, now
tacking away, embroidering the field
free-style, because it must.

*

Far from the indifferent North,
my love and fury flourish
in the self-same southern latitude.
Out of the stuff of longing they give
birth to themselves in different writing;
but would he understand how
inseparable they are, my siamese twins
love and rage, joined at the heart?

\*

How can the woman who loves
and the woman who writes poems about it
and the woman who writes about writing
about loving someone who might be him
walk the same wire together?

\*

I won't give them up,
the thoughts he finds 'too much',
strings slung across absences.

But the gods have chosen him
to teach me paradox: already
I've let go what I never had.

Soon, feckless as a thrush, and as repetitive,
I'll perch so lightly in his branches
my song won't agitate a single leaf.

\*

When he's exhausted, I want to author his sleep,
build a perfectly shaped stanza for him to rest in.
Don't tell me – I know the avarice of giving;
how even a baby sleeps its own sleep entirely.
I used to fidget round my unconscious child,
sing within earshot, greedy to be necessary again.

\*

We're dancing a tango.
  I'm coming to trust
    his pace, his distance
      from the vertical.

      At this angle, nothing for it
        but to give myself
          to the invention
            uncertainty releases:

            dialect we forge
              from closeness, breaks;
                hieroglyphs
                  on earth and air.

                  And what can be said
                    isn't the half of it.

                                    *

All that turbulence,
the prickling static
of old clingy habits;

all those high-priced,
uncomfortable garments
I've thought were love.

On a long out-breath,
one by one by one,
I let them drop.

They creep back, of course,
over my chest, solar plexus.
I'm patient with them,

knowing how it is;
breathe out, let them
fall away again. Again.

Only then, uncovered,
can I begin to call things
by their proper names.

        *

Love: a clear pool, a kingfisher
flashing across, reflected.

Once seen, the kingfisher can't be un-seen
– it blesses the inward eye perpetually.

It may be rare, elusive. It may
prize the free air above everything.

But water holds awareness of the grace,
the brilliance, and is changed for good.

# Notes

**Forgiveness**: Silver becomes stressed and brittle when overworked. Annealing, which involves both heating and cooling, restores it to a more resilient condition.

**The Life and Life of Henrietta Lacks**: Henrietta Lacks died in 1951, but her cells, amounting to several times her original weight, live on in laboratories around the world.

**The Woman Next Door**: Eva Fogelman: *Conscience and Courage: Rescuers of Jews during the Holocaust* (Victor Gollancz, 1995).

**Undine**: Undine: spirit of the waters, created without a soul. By marrying a mortal and bearing his child, she acquired a soul and, with it, human frailties and sensibilities.

**Constanze's Wedding**: *Oh I loved, I was so happy!*, sung by Constanze in *Die Entführung aus dem Serail,* written in the year of Mozart's marriage to Constanze Weber.

**Jacques Lacan's Table**: Lacan was a French psychoanalyst, originator of the concept of the 'mirror stage' of child development.

**Love and Variations**: *scordatura*: abnormal tuning of stringed instrument, e.g. for the purpose of increasing the compass.